The Thai (

The Asian Testkitchen

Published by Mindful
Publishing

TABLE OF CONTENT

Thai Green Curry Chicken

Laab Gai - Thai chicken salad

Fried Morning Glory

Thai spring rolls - Po Piah

Kaeng phet - classic red Thai curry

Beef with green beans, spicy

Gold bag - Tung Thong

Thai - minced beef salad

Thai cucumber salad with peanuts and chili

Vegan Thai curry glass noodle soup

Red chicken curry

Thai peanut chicken with fine chili

Pad Krapao Gai

Saté skewers with chicken

Spicy beef salad

Massaman Curry

Thai glass noodle salad - Yam Woon Sen

Fast Thai curry with chicken, paprika and a fine peanut note

Thai coconut soup with chicken

Thai Curry

Tom Kha Gai - the famous chicken soup with coconut milk and galangal

Stuffed Thai omelet

Thai curry with chicken, snow peas and mango

Thai curry with prawns and sweet potatoes

Gai Jang - Thai grilled chicken

Peanut Sauce

Panäng Moo

Pineapple - Sauce

Paprika - coconut - curry with turkey and rice

Thai Lychee Curry

Light chicken curry with lemongrass

Thai fish from the grill

South Thai curry with prawns and pineapple

Thai chicken sweet-sour

Pad Cha with different seafood or fish

THAI RED CURRY

666 kcal
Working time approx. 30 minutes
cooking / baking time approx. 20 minutes
Total time approx. 50 minutes

ingredients
300 g meat or fish of your choice
1 tablespoon curry paste, red
1 glass of water
400 ml coconut milk
800 g vegetables of your choice
2 tablespoons fish sauce
2 tablespoons soy sauce, light
1 tablespoon palm sugar or brown cane sugar
2 peppers, red or green, cut diagonally
2 chili pepper(s), small hot (as desired)
6 leaves Thai basil, fresh
2 tablespoons rapeseed oil or peanut oil

Preparation
This basic recipe can be varied according to your
mood by varying the meat (e.g. chicken breast,
turkey breast, beef tenderloin or pork tenderloin)
or with fish fillet or shrimps and with various

vegetables (e.g. bamboo sprouts in strips, soybean sprouts, carrots, baby corn, sugar snap peas, Thai eggplants, pak choi, etc.) to create an ever new pleasure experience. Let your creativity run free! It is also suitable for vegetarians, as it can be prepared exclusively with many different vegetables.

The dish does not have to be prepared in a wok, it works just as well in a wide pot, because it has soup character.

Sauté the curry paste in hot oil, add a little water, add the coconut milk little by little and always stir well before adding more (gives a very nice red color). Cut the intended meat (fish or shrimps) into bite-sized pieces, add them and let them simmer for about 5 minutes until they are done. Shrimps only need a very short time!

Add the vegetables of your choice cut into strips (no matter which and how many varieties) and bring everything back to the boil. Everything should remain firm to the bite and keep its color (add Pak Choi or Chinese cabbage only shortly before the end).

Season to taste with the fish sauce, light soy sauce and palm sugar. Add Thai basil leaves and pepperoni, continue cooking for another minute. Add the chopped chili rolls to taste and season to taste.

Serve hot with rice (basmati, jasmine rice or Thai scented rice)

SPICY THAI SOUP WITH COCONUT AND CHICKEN

Working time approx. 20 minutes
cooking / baking time approx. 10 minutes
Total time approx. 30 minutes

ingredients
300 g chicken breast, diced
1 bunch spring onion(s)
2 cm ginger, fresh or 2 teaspoons ground
1 liter chicken broth
1 can of coconut milk
3 tablespoons soy sauce
2 teaspoons curry paste, red or green
1 bell pepper(s), red, diced
100 g mushrooms, diced
1 stem lemon grass or 1 - 2 teaspoons dried
1 chili pepper(s), fresh or dried, chopped
125 g Chinese egg noodles
1 tablespoon of oil
1 handful coriander green, freshly cut

salt and pepper
possibly chili threads for garnishing

Preparation
Cut the chicken into small pieces and roast it briefly in the pot. Cut the spring onions into rings and the ginger into small pieces. Add both and fry briefly.

Then deglaze with the chicken broth. Add coconut milk, soy sauce and curry paste. Cut the lemongrass lengthwise crosswise so that it remains in one piece, so that you can remove it later and add it to the soup.

Cook for 5 minutes, then add the remaining vegetables and spices. Add the noodles (cooking time according to package instructions).

If you like, you can pick up some fresh coriander and sprinkle it over the soup at the end. From time to time I still use dried chili threads for garnishing.

TOM KA GAI - SOUP

Total time approx. 45 minutes

ingredients
500 g chicken breast fillet
2 can/s of coconut milk (400 ml each)
250 ml vegetable broth
2 stems lemon grass
1 large onion(s)
3 clove/s of garlic
1 chili pepper(s), red
5 teaspoons Tom Ka-Paste, red
1 glass bamboo shoot(s)
20 g ginger, fresh
2 bunches coriander green
1 dash of soy sauce
possibly sauce thickener

Preparation
To prepare, cut the chicken fillet into small pieces. Finely chop or crush the onion and garlic. Remove the seeds from the chili pepper and cut into fine

strips. Peel and finely chop the ginger.

First of all, let the onion in the pot run glassy. Then add the garlic and the Tom Ka paste. Then add vegetable stock and coconut milk and bring to the boil.

Add lemongrass, chili pepper and ginger to the pot and bring to the boil again. Then add the chicken meat and simmer for about 5 minutes, stirring occasionally. Then add the bamboo shoots and season with salt and lemon juice. Do not use too much salt, because already the Tom Ka paste is very spicy.

Remove the lemongrass sticks from the soup again (they are tough, should only give off the taste). Let the soup steep for a few more minutes and then serve sprinkled with coriander.

THAI SHRIMP AND POTATO SOUP

Working time approx. 20 minutes
cooking / baking time approx. 25 minutes
Total time approx. 45 minutes

ingredients
1 large potato(es)
1 small onion(s)
1 piece ginger root
800 ml vegetable broth, approx.
coconut milk at will
1 teaspoon curry powder
½ teaspoon turmeric
4 shrimp(s)
Coriander
1 lime(s)

Preparation
Fry the finely chopped onion and ginger in oil. Add
the potatoes cut into small pieces and fry them.
Then dust with curry and turmeric and top up with
vegetable stock and coconut milk. Let it cook for

about 20 minutes.

When the soup has cooled down a bit, puree every-thing in a food processor or with a blender. Put it back into the pot and season with salt, pepper and lime juice. Finally, let the prawns soak for 1 minute, just a short time, otherwise they will get hard.

Serve sprinkled with finely chopped coriander.

The amount of ingredients varies according to taste.

YAM TALEH - THAI - SALAD WITH SEAFOOD

Total time approx. 40 minutes

ingredients
500 g seafood, mixed, prepared ready to cook
5 shallot(s) (Thai shallots)
1 piece ginger, fresh, approx. 5 cm
2 chili pepper(s), green (or more if required)
2 chili pepper(s), red (or more if required)
1 handful of mint (fresh leaves)
5 stems of celery (Thai celery)
3 stems lemongrass
4 tablespoons lime juice
2 tablespoons fish sauce
some chili powder or chili flakes
½ teaspoon sugar
some salad, some leaves of it

Preparation
Peel and chop the Thai shallots. Peel and grate the

ginger. Chop the chillies. Pluck the mint leaves from the stalks and chop them (leave some for garnishing). Cut the Thai celery into 5 cm long pieces. Cut the lemongrass (only the white inner one) into very fine rings.

Prepare the seafood, mix with fish sauce and lime juice and then cook in a wok until cooked (takes about 5 minutes).

Mix the remaining ingredients - except for the lettuce leaves and the whole mint leaves - well and pour over the seafood, which has cooled down somewhat in the meantime. Mix everything well and season to taste with the spices. Arrange the salad on the lettuce leaves and serve garnished with the whole mint leaves.

THAI - CURRY POWDER

Total time approx. 20 minutes

ingredients
2 teaspoons cloves
5 cm cinnamon, whole
2 teaspoons fennel seeds
4 bay leaves
2 tablespoons cumin
5 tablespoons coriander
2 teaspoons turmeric
2 teaspoons paprika powder, rose hot, or more

Preparation
Place all the ingredients in a wok or pan. Without adding fat, roast at medium temperature for about 1 min. while stirring until the mixture smells aromatic. Allow to cool and then grind finely in a mortar, mix well and pour into glasses, ready.

You get about 10 tablespoons of homemade curry powder. Sealed in a glass, the curry powder keeps its aroma for up to one year. And the nice thing is, you can determine yourself, which sharpness the powder should have.

THAI CURRY WITH MASSAMAN

Working time approx. 30 minutes
cooking / baking time approx. 35 minutes
Total time approx. 1 hour 5 minutes

ingredients
200 g chicken breast fillet
1 teaspoon, heaped cornstarch
4 tablespoons peanut oil
40 g cashew nuts
1 garlic clove(s)
1 tablespoon, heaped curry paste (Massaman)
2 onion(s)
400 ml coconut milk
250 ml chicken broth
2 small potato(es), firm boiling
1 teaspoon tamarind paste
1 teaspoon palm sugar
3 tablespoons fish sauce
chili flakes at will
2 slice/s of pineapple, fresh
2 spring onion(s)

Preparation
Wash and pat the chicken breast fillet dry, cut into strips and place on a plate. Do not season. Dust with cornflour and knead it carefully into the meat so that the meat is covered with it.

Peel, wash and quarter the potatoes. Peel and quarter the onions. Peel and finely dice the garlic clove.

Fry the cashew nuts in some oil and pour it on a kitchen paper. In the same pan, fry the meat until crispy with 1 tablespoon of peanut oil and put it on a paper towel.

Wash the spring onions and cut only the greenery into 1 cm wide rings, use the rest for other purposes. Peel the fresh pineapple and cut 2 slices into small pieces. (The cashew nuts, the meat, the spring onions and the pineapple pieces are added to the sauce only at the end).

Add 2 tablespoons of oil to the pan and lightly roast the garlic over medium heat. Add the curry paste and also fry a little. Add the onions and fry. Deglaze the mixture with the coconut milk and the chicken stock. Add the potatoes, tamarind paste, palm sugar and fish sauce and let the sauce simmer at medium heat until the potatoes are done and the sauce has the desired consistency. If necessary add some more broth.

Now add the meat, pineapple pieces, cashew nuts

and spring onions and let it simmer gently for another 2 minutes. Season the curry to taste and if necessary add chili flakes for spiciness.

Thai fragrant rice and as a drink a Singha beer goes well with it.

THAI CHICKEN WITH CASHEW NUTS

Working time approx. 15 minutes
cooking / baking time approx. 25 minutes
Total time approx. 40 minutes

ingredients
300 g chicken breast
½ cup cashew nuts, unroasted, unsalted
1 small onion(s), diced
2 clove/s of garlic, chopped
5 large chili pepper(s), dried, cut into 1.5 cm pieces
3 spring onion(s), cut into 3 cm pieces
some flour
1 tablespoon Sriracha sauce
2 tablespoons oyster sauce
1 tablespoon of sugar
1 tablespoon soy sauce
1 tablespoon fish sauce (Nam Pla)
2 teaspoons sesame oil
3 tablespoons of water

2 cup/s of oil, for frying (e.g. peanut oil)

Preparation

Cut the chicken breast into pieces, drizzle with a little soy sauce and let it soak in for a few minutes, then cover with flour, not too thick.

Heat oil in a wok and fry the chicken pieces until they are light brown and crispy, then take them out and put them on kitchen paper.

Fry the raw cashew nuts on a low flame in the same oil until light brown. The oil must not be too hot, otherwise the nuts become bitter. Take them out and fry the chillies in the same oil for a few minutes without burning them.

In a bowl, mix srracha, oyster sauce, sugar, soy sauce, fish sauce, sesame oil and water.

Drain the oil from the wok to 2 tablespoons. Heat the wok again and roast the garlic briefly, then add the onions and sauté. Add the meat again, then the sauce mixture, stir a little, then add the cashew nuts, chili and spring onions and fry everything for 1 - 2 minutes.

Serve with rice.

BIHUN - SOUP

Total time approx. 30 minutes

ingredients
1 stick/s of celery
1 stick/s of spring onion(s)
1 stick/s of leek (rather thin)
1 bell bell pepper(s), red
200 g mushrooms, fresh or canned
1 glass of chicken broth
1 teaspoon Sambal Oelek
1 pack of glass noodles (Soeoen Laksa)
450 g turkey escalope
2 tablespoons soy sauce
1 pinch(s) of salt
1 pinch(s) of pepper
some oil for roasting
some water as needed

Preparation
First cut the turkey meat into small pieces. In a bowl, mix with 2-3 tablespoons of soy sauce and place in the refrigerator.
In the meantime, wash the vegetables. Thinly slice the leek, spring onion and celery. Cut the red bell

pepper into small cubes (rather thinly), cut the mushrooms into thin slices.

Use a large pot, add some oil to the pot and roast the marinated meat. Add the vegetables and steam. Deglaze with the chicken broth, add some more water and season with salt and pepper. Add Sambal Oelek (be careful, because it becomes more intense and spicy by boiling) and let it boil for about 25 minutes.

Put glass noodles in an extra bowl and soak them with cold water for about 10 minutes. Then add to the boiling broth (drain well beforehand) and cook for another 2-3 minutes.

Serve hot.

SPICY HONEY CHICKEN

867 kcal
Working time approx. 15 minutes
Rest period approx. 12 hours
Total time approx. 12 hours 15 minutes

ingredients
1 chicken, ready to cook and cut
4 clove/s of garlic, roughly chopped
3 tablespoons Sambal Oelek
2 tablespoons honey
2 tablespoons soy sauce
2 teaspoons sugar, brown
2 tablespoons of oil

Preparation
Mix the ingredients to a marinade and add to the chicken. Leave to stand in the refrigerator for a few hours, covered, preferably overnight. Cook in the oven on the grill at 180 degrees, after half of the baking time (approx. 45 min) cover again with the remaining marinade. Important! Push the juice bowl

under the grill and cover it with aluminium foil, otherwise the washing up will become a mess!

THAI CURRY WITH CHICKEN BREAST AND COCONUT MILK

Total time approx. 30 minutes

ingredients
500 g chicken breast fillet
2 tablespoons soy sauce
1 tablespoon of sugar
Pepper
1 garlic clove(s)
800 g vegetables, mixed to taste
1 glass bamboo shoot(s), in strips
½ Tin of coconut milk
1 tablespoon curry paste, green

Preparation
Cut the chicken breast into strips and marinate in a marinade of soy sauce, pepper and sugar for about 1 hour.

Roast well in the wok or pan. Remove.

Wash and finely chop the mixed vegetables and bamboo sprouts, also roast, then remove.

Mix the curry paste and the coconut milk in the wok and let it simmer for a short time (!). Then add the meat and vegetables again and let it simmer briefly. Season to taste with soy sauce.

Chinese sticky rice goes well with it.

THAI COCONUT-VEGETABLE-CHICKEN-CURRY

1333 kcal
Working time approx. 15 minutes
cooking / baking time approx. 15 minutes
Total time approx. 30 minutes

ingredients
150 g basmati rice
salt and pepper
some chili powder
300 g chicken breast
some oil for frying
1 medium zucchini
1 large bell bell pepper(s), red
1 medium carrot(s)
½ Onion(s)
1 teaspoon curry paste, red
½ Clove/n garlic
some ginger
400 ml coconut milk

1 handful of cashew nuts

Preparation
Prepare the basmati rice according to the instructions on the packet.

Cut the chicken breast into pieces and season with some salt, pepper and chili powder. Heat the oil in a large pan and roast the meat in it.

Cut the zucchini, peppers and carrot into pieces, add them to the chicken breast in the pan and roast them as well. Cut the onion, some garlic and some ginger into small pieces, add them to the red curry paste in the pan and fry them briefly. Deglaze with the coconut milk and if necessary add some water or cow's milk to get the desired consistency. Season to taste with red curry paste, chili powder, salt and pepper.

Sprinkle with cashew nuts and serve with the rice.

RED THAI CURRY WITH CHICKEN

Working time approx. 25 minutes
cooking / baking time approx. 25 minutes
Total time approx. 50 minutes

ingredients
250 g Basmati
600 g chicken breast fillet
2 bunches spring onion(s)
200 g carrot(s)
2 tablespoons of oil
Salt
50 g curry paste, red
2 can/s of coconut milk
2 tablespoons peanuts, unsalted
Sugar

Preparation
Cook the rice in salt water. Cut meat into cubes, spring onions into rings and carrots into slices.

Heat oil. Roast meat and carrots in it, add spring onions and a little salt. Stir in curry paste, deglaze with coconut milk and simmer a little.

In the meantime chop the nuts. Season the curry with salt and sugar and serve sprinkled with peanuts. Serve with rice.

SPICY CHICKEN - NOODLE SOUP

822 kcal
Total time approx. 20 minutes

ingredients
125 g Chinese egg noodles
1 tablespoon of oil
4 chicken legs, without skin and bones
1 bunch spring onion(s), sliced
2 clove/s of garlic, chopped
2 cm ginger, fresh, finely chopped
850 ml chicken broth
200 ml coconut milk
3 teaspoons curry paste, red
3 tablespoons peanut butter
2 tablespoons soy sauce
1 small bell pepper(s), red, diced
60 g peas, frozen
salt and pepper

Preparation
Soften the pasta in a bowl of boiling water (for about

3-4 minutes).

Heat the oil in a pot or large wok. Add the diced chicken meat and fry for 5 minutes until it is lightly browned. Add the white pieces of spring onions, garlic and ginger, stir well and fry for 2 minutes. Add the broth, coconut milk, curry paste, peanut butter and soy sauce, season with salt and pepper and bring to a boil. Stir and simmer for 8 minutes.

Stir from time to time. Add peppers, peas and the green pieces of spring onions and simmer for another 2 minutes. Add the drained noodles to the soup and heat. Serve the soup in warmed bowls. If you don't like it that hot, just use green curry paste.

THAI CHILI SAUCE

538 kcal
Total time approx. 30 minutes

ingredients
5 Thai chili pepper(s), fresh red, medium hot
3 clove(s) of garlic
30 g ginger root, fresh
100 g sugar
3 tablespoons vinegar, lighter
2 teaspoons cornstarch
Salt

Preparation
Wash the chilies, cut them into quarters lengthwise and cut them into small pieces together with the seeds. Peel the ginger and garlic and chop very finely.

Put the sugar in a pot and moisten it with some water. Melt at medium heat. Sauté the garlic and chilies for about 5 minutes. Remove the pot from the heat and let it cool down briefly. Add the ginger, pour on 1/4 l water and bring to the boil while stirring. Mix the cornflour with some cold water, pour the vinegar into the syrup and let everything boil gently for about 3 minutes. Salt and let cool down.

THAI GREEN CURRY CHICKEN

Working time approx. 15 minutes
cooking / baking time approx. 15 minutes
Total time approx. 30 minutes

ingredients
500 g chicken breast fillet
1 zucchini
6 Thai eggplant(s)
1 bell bell pepper(s), green, cleaned
broccoli, some florets
3 Kaffir lime leaves
1 handful Thai basil, sweet
2 Thai chili pepper(s), fresh green
3 tablespoons peanut oil
2 tablespoons curry paste, green
1 tablespoon soy sauce
1 tablespoon fish sauce
2 tablespoons sugar, brown or palm sugar, approx.
1 can of coconut milk

Preparation

Cut the chicken breast fillet into small bite-sized pieces. Cut the vegetables into small pieces as well, but eggplants only later, as they turn brown very quickly. You can steam the broccoli first, it tastes better.

Heat peanut oil in a large pan, add green curry paste and mix, deglaze with some coconut milk. Add chicken and fry it, add green chilies and then vegetables and fry it depending on how long it takes to cook. Add sugar, soy sauce and fish sauce and deglaze everything again with coconut milk. I prefer a thick sauce, so I add the coconut milk little by little until I reach the desired consistency.

Now add the lime leaves, simmer for about 3 - 5 minutes, then add the Thai basil leaves. Remove from heat immediately and serve with Thai jasmine rice.

A well chilled beer tastes good with it.

This recipe is really very tasty, but for people who have not had much experience with exotic dishes, it takes getting used to. It is also really hot, because the paste is already made of chilies, for sensitive eaters leave out the fresh chilies.

LAAB GAI - THAI CHICKEN SALAD

Total time approx. 20 minutes

ingredients
300 g chicken breast
1 lime(s), possibly 2, juice thereof
2 stem(s) of lemongrass
1 tablespoon fish sauce
1 teaspoon of sugar
½ teaspoon chili flakes
3 cm galangal or ginger
3 shallot(s) (Thai shallots, alternatively 1 small onion)
3 stems of celery (Thai celery, alternatively 1 - 2 stems of native celery)
4 spring onion(s) (Thai spring onions, alternatively 2 - 3 native spring onions)
½ bunch coriander green
1 stem of mint, more according to taste
2 chilli pepper(s), red, more according to taste
1 cucumber(s)
some leaf salad

Preparation

Dice the chicken breast either very finely with a knife or chop it into small pieces with a meat cleaver, similar to coarse minced meat. Mix the meat with lime juice and marinate for about 10 - 15 minutes. Without adding any fat, roast it in a pan until it is hot and ready to cook. The liquid in the pan should have evaporated.

In the meantime, cut the soft part of the lemon grass very finely, dice the galangal finely. Finely chop the shallots, celery, spring onions, coriander, mint and chillies and put everything aside.

Season the chicken with fish sauce, sugar and chili flakes. If necessary, add lime juice and let it cool down lukewarm. Now mix the meat with the shallots, herbs, etc. and arrange on salad leaves. Cut the cucumber into slices or longitudinal strips and serve together with the rennet and jasmine rice.

Sprinkle 1 - 2 tablespoons of rice semolina over the finished rennet as desired. Rice semolina can easily be made by carefully roasting raw rice grains in a pan without fat until golden yellow. Stir constantly, then let it cool down and crush it in a mortar (grain size like coarse semolina). The rice semolina can be kept for several months in a closed jar.

FRIED MORNING GLORY

Working time approx. 15 minutes
cooking / baking time approx. 2 minutes
Total time approx. 17 minutes

ingredients
400 g spinach (Morning Glory - Thai water spinach)
10 clove/s of garlic
6 chilli pepper(s), Thai, long, red (Prik Chee fah Sot Daeng), to taste
2 tablespoons soybeans, yellow, salted, from the jar
1 tablespoon fish sauce
1 tablespoon oyster sauce
1 teaspoon sugar, brown
some vegetable oil

Preparation
Wash Morning Glory and break the leaves off the stems. Cut the stalks into pieces of about 5 cm length. Chop the garlic, cut the chillies into rings (you can also leave out chillies without any problems), rinse yellow beans well.

Heat oil in a wok. When the oil is hot, add garlic and after a few seconds the stems. Stir for about 1 minute, then add all other ingredients, stir quickly, season to taste and remove from heat. Quickly put it on a plate, otherwise it will recook.

Serve as a side dish with other Thai dishes and rice.

If you prefer, you can crush garlic and chilies in a mortar and roast them first in hot oil, then continue as described above.

THAI SPRING ROLLS - PO PIAH

Total time approx. 1 hour 15 minutes

ingredients
1 tablespoon of oil
300 g minced pork meat, lean
4 garlic clove(s), finely chopped
6 spring onion(s) (Thai), chopped, the white and green separately
2 small carrot(s), finely rasped
100 g white cabbage, very finely cut or:
100 g sprouts (mung bean sprouts), roughly chopped
10 medium-sized mushrooms (tongo, shitake, dried), soaked in hot water for 30 minutes
100 g glass noodles, soaked in hot water for 10 minutes
3 tablespoons oyster sauce
2 tablespoons fish sauce
2 tablespoons soy sauce, light
1 teaspoon of sugar
Pepper, black, freshly ground
40 dough - leaves for spring rolls, deep-frozen

1 liter of oil, for frying
Lettuce, (leaf or iceberg lettuce)
For the set:
Cucumber(s) and coriander

For the sauce:
6 tablespoons lime juice
2 tablespoons palm sugar, grated
1 tablespoon fish sauce
2 tablespoons shallot(s), Thai red, very finely diced
1 tablespoon chili pepper(s), green and red, without seeds, cut into tiny cubes

Preparation
Fry the garlic and the white of the spring onions briefly in oil, add the minced meat and fry until crumbly, lightly golden brown. Mix in the prepared vegetables and mushrooms and fry for 2-3 minutes. Stir in the seasoning sauces, pepper and sugar and season to taste. Let cool slightly and mix in the glass noodles. Season the filling to taste again. It should now be as dry as possible, otherwise pour off the liquid.

Meanwhile, remove the pastry sheets from the package and cover them with a damp cloth so that they do not dry out when defrosted.

Place one sheet of dough on each work surface with the tip facing down. Place a heaped tablespoon of filling on the lower third, beat the tip of the sheet about one third over the mixture, press well and roll it up tightly once. Now fold the two sides tightly to the middle and roll up to the end.

Mix 1 tablespoon of flour with a little water to a paste. Put a small spot on the top of each dough sheet and close the roll with it.

Place on a plate. Do not stack the prepared rolls or store them for a long time, otherwise the dough can soak through.

Heat the oil in a wok and fry the rolls until golden brown. Drain them on kitchen paper and keep them side by side in the oven at 70 degrees Celsius for only a short time. They taste best fresh from the wok.

Arrange on salad leaves and serve immediately. Serve with the dip sauce.

For the dip sauce, mix all the ingredients until the palm sugar is completely dissolved.

If you find chilies too hot, you can also use pepperoni. If you prefer it hotter, add a few chili peppers to the dip.

Note:
This is a variation of the usual Thai spring rolls, which consist of raw vegetables and cooked chicken, pork or shrimp meat.

The advantage of this variation is that the rolls can be frozen raw very well. They taste much better after deep-frying than those with raw vegetables.

KAENG PHET
- CLASSIC RED
THAI CURRY

Working time approx. 15 minutes
cooking / baking time approx. 15 minutes
Total time approx. 30 minutes

ingredients
½ Liters of coconut milk
0.1 liter coconut cream, possibly, and for that cor-
respondingly less coconut milk
1 tablespoon curry paste, red
200 g meat, fish, shrimps or tofu
2 tablespoons fish sauce
2 tablespoons palm sugar
100 g eggplant(s) (Thai eggplant)
100 g bamboo shoot(s)
Mushrooms, optional
Bell pepper(s), optional
5 Kaffir lime leaves
3 sprig(s) of Thai basil, sweet,
1 chili pepper(s) (Thai chili)

1 stem(s) of lemongrass
some peanut oil for frying

Preparation
Fry the red curry paste in peanut oil in a wok over a high heat to ignite the full aroma of the paste. Then deglaze the curry paste with 500 ml coconut milk. If you prefer a creamier taste, you can also replace 100 ml of the coconut milk with the same amount of coconut cream. Boil up the coconut milk and add the meat (or fish, shrimp or tofu), fish sauce and palm sugar. Put the stove down and let the previous ingredients simmer for 5 minutes at low heat.

Remove the stalk of the Thai eggplant and cut it into quarters or eights. Add the Thai eggplant, the bamboo shoots and possibly other vegetables - peppers, mushrooms, etc. - Add them and let them simmer for another two minutes.

Cut the kaffir lime leaves into strips. Cut the Thai chili into rings. Cut the lemon grass into about 10 rings, according to taste. Add the kaffir lime leaves, Thai chili and basil leaves and let the dish simmer for one minute more.

Serve the curry with rice.

BEEF WITH GREEN BEANS, SPICY

260 kcal
Working time approx. 20 minutes
Rest period approx. 1 hour
cooking / baking time approx. 15 minutes
Total time approx. 1 hour 35 minutes

ingredients
400 g beef, tender, for short roast, e.g. fillet, loin or rump
6 tablespoons soy sauce
½ Teaspoon pepper, black
400 g beans, green
2 tablespoons curry paste, red
2 tablespoons fish sauce
3 stems lemongrass
3 tablespoons of sugar
5 tablespoons of oil

Preparation
Wash the beef, dab dry and cut into strips. Mix with
3 tablespoons of soy sauce and pepper and marinate

covered in the refrigerator for about 1 hour.

Meanwhile, clean the beans and cut them into 4 cm long pieces. Bring a pot of water to a boil and blanch the beans in boiling water for about 8 minutes. Drain and rinse with cold water.

Chop lemon grass very finely, mix with curry paste, 3 tablespoons of soy sauce, fish sauce and sugar.

Heat the oil in a wok and fry the beef briefly, then reduce the heat, add the beans and deglaze with the sauce. Steam for another 1 minute.

Serve with rice.

GOLD BAG - TUNG THONG

Total time approx. 30 minutes

ingredients
250 g minced pork meat, lean
3 small mushrooms, tongo mushrooms (shitake, dried), soaked in hot water for 30 minutes
1 medium-sized carrot(s), finely grated
1 tablespoon coriander root, cleaned and finely chopped
1 tablespoon coriander green, chopped
1 teaspoon garlic, finely chopped
2 small spring onions, finely chopped
1 chili pepper(s), red, seeded, finely chopped (possibly omitted)
1 egg
1 tablespoon fish sauce
1 tablespoon soy sauce, light
Pepper, black
Sugar
Salt
25 dough - leaves (Wantan) or for spring rolls

Chives, briefly blanched
Oil, for frying
sauce, pineapple sauce, plum sauce or
Chilli sauce, sweet and sour

Preparation
For the filling, crush the garlic and coriander roots with the pepper.
Squeeze the mushrooms and cut them into fine strips, removing the stalk. Finely dice the strips.
Mix minced pork, egg, diced mushrooms, grated carrots, coriander greens and the chopped spring onions with the paste and season to taste with fish sauce, soy sauce, pepper, salt and sugar.
Place a wonton leaf in the hollow of your hand, put a teaspoon of mixture in the middle and press the leaf together to form a sachet. Tie together with a chive stalk and decoratively pull apart the edges of the dough. (Thin blanched leek strips are also suitable as an alternative).
Heat the oil in a wok and fry the bags in it until golden brown and crispy.
Drain on kitchen paper and serve hot with pineapple sauce, plum sauce and/or sweet-and-sour chilli sauce.

Alternative: Replace the minced pork with chopped raw shrimp. Then this appetizer is called a silver pouch.

THAI – MINCED BEEF SALAD

Total time approx. 30 minutes

ingredients
500 g minced meat (beef)
1 lime(s), the juice thereof
8 shallot(s) (red Thai shallots)
1 piece galangal, fresh, approx. 2 cm
5 Kaffir lime leaves (Magrood leaves)
3 stems coriander without root
2 stems of mint, only the leaves of it
4 tablespoons fish sauce, a few splashes of tamarind juice if required
1 tablespoon palm sugar, crushed
1 teaspoon chili powder (more if needed)
2 chili pepper(s) (Thai long-red chilies)
3 tablespoons of semolina (rice semolina of fragrant rice), freshly roasted, not too finely ground

Preparation
Mix the minced beef well with the lime juice and let it soak for about 10 minutes.

Peel the shallots and cut into fine slices. Peel the galangal and chop it as fine as possible. Roll up the Magrood leaves and cut into fine strips. Core the chillies and cut them into strips. Coarsely chop the prepared coriander and mint leaves (put some of the leaves aside for decoration).
With the coriander, it is not tragic to chop some of the stems.

Heat a pan without oil. Add the minced meat and stir-fry over medium heat for about 5 - 7 minutes, adding a few drops of tamarind juice (if necessary). Remove the pan from the heat and season with fish sauce, palm sugar, chili powder and possibly some lime juice as well. Stir well. Fold in rice semolina, Magrood leaf strips, shallots, red chillies, galangal and the herbs.

Decorate with the set aside coriander and mint leaves and serve lukewarm.

THAI CUCUMBER SALAD WITH PEANUTS AND CHILI

204 kcal
Working time approx. 25 minutes
Rest period approx. 1 hour
Total time approx. 1 hour 25 minutes

ingredients
3 medium sized cucumber(s)
2 tablespoons white wine vinegar or rice vinegar
2 teaspoons sugar
2 tablespoons chili sauce, e.g. sweet-hot
1 onion(s), red
Coriander green, fresh
100 g peanuts
2 tablespoons garlic
1 teaspoon chili pepper(s), chopped
1 tablespoon fish sauce

Preparation

Peel and halve the cucumbers and scrape out the seeds with a small spoon. Cut the cucumber halves into slices. Peel onion and cut into half rings, add to the cucumbers.

Mix vinegar and sugar well and pour over the cucumbers and onions together with the chili sauce and coriander. Mix everything well and let it stand for about 45 minutes.

Chop the garlic very small and fry it in a pan without fat until golden brown.

Then chop the peanuts coarsely and roast them also without fat. Put aside.

Shortly before serving, mix the peanuts, garlic, chili pepper and the fish sauce and add to the salad. If necessary, season again with vinegar and chili sauce.

VEGAN THAI CURRY GLASS NOODLE SOUP

Working time approx. 20 minutes
cooking / baking time approx. 15 minutes
Total time approx. 35 minutes

ingredients
800 ml vegetable broth
400 ml coconut milk
2 pak choi
2 clove(s) of garlic
1 sweet potato(es)
2 tablespoons curry paste, red
1 tablespoon lime juice
1 tablespoon soy sauce
1 teaspoon ginger, ground
100 g glass noodles
1 handful of coriander leaves
1 handful of bean sprouts
1 onion(s), red

Preparation

Cut the Pak Choi into strips and put the green part aside. Chop the garlic cloves and the coriander finely, dice the sweet potato. Halve the onion and cut into slices.

Heat some oil in a large pot and sauté the garlic until transparent. Add the ginger and curry paste and sweat along as well. Deglaze with the vegetable stock. Add the diced sweet potatoes and the white part of the pak choi and cook for 5 minutes.

Add the coconut milk, soy sauce and lemon juice and mix well. Add the noodles and the green part of the pak choi and bring to the boil for another 3 minutes.

Divide into bowls and garnish with coriander, bean sprouts and onion slices.

RED CHICKEN CURRY

Total time approx. 30 minutes

ingredients
600 g chicken breast fillet
1 bell bell pepper(s), red
5 spring onion(s)
1 clove/n garlic
4 Kaffir lime leaves (Magrood leaves)
1 can/s of coconut milk, unshaken (400 ml)
2 tablespoons curry paste, red
3 tablespoons fish sauce
1 tablespoon lime juice
3 tablespoons palm sugar or brown cane sugar
1 bunch basil, horopa (sweet Thai basil)

Preparation
Cut chicken breast fillet into strips against the fiber. I never cut the meat strips too fine, but also not so big that they hang over the spoon. Cut the bell bell pepper into quarters and also crosswise into strips and the spring onions crosswise into about 1 cm pieces.

From the Magrood leaves cut out the inner leaf stalk and cut into very fine strips, finely chop garlic.
Wash, shake off and dry the basil.

Heat up the wok. From the unshaken tin on top, add approx. 3-4 tablespoons of the settled coconut cream and let it boil for approx. 1 minute, under supervision and stirring, then mix the curry paste with a whisk. Let this mixture simmer until small bubbles appear and discolour and smell at the edges. Now add the garlic and the Magrood leaves and roast again briefly.

Then add the rest of the coconut milk, bring to the boil and simmer for about 15 minutes, until small globules of fat appear.

Season to taste with the fish sauce, sugar and lime juice.

Now first add the meat and let it simmer at medium heat for about 5 minutes, then put the spring onions together with the paprika in the wok and let it simmer for about 5 minutes with the pot closed.
Only shortly before serving stir in the plucked Horopa leaves and serve with Thai fragrant rice.

THAI PEANUT CHICKEN WITH FINE CHILI

Working time approx. 20 minutes
cooking / baking time approx. 4 hours
Total time approx. 4 hours 20 minutes

ingredients
4 chicken breast fillet, diced (max. 2 x 2 cm)
1 large bell pepper(s), red, cut into strips
1 bunch spring onion(s), cut into not too fine rings
150 g peanut cream
125 ml chicken broth, seasoned
3 tablespoons soy sauce
3 tablespoons chili sauce, hot
3 tablespoons honey
½ Lemon(s), juice thereof
¼ teaspoon cumin powder
1 garlic clove(s), pressed through
1 teaspoon ginger, grated
salt and pepper

Preparation
First we put the chicken as well as the paprika and spring onion in the ceramic pot and mix it briefly. From the remaining ingredients we prepare a cold stirred sauce, which is poured directly over the ingredients.

Braising time (in a 200 watt appliance): 1 hour HIGH and 3 hours LOW.

It is recommended to stir thoroughly once after approx. 2 hours, as the chicken cubes like to stick together. Finally, season with salt and pepper or with the sauce ingredients.

I serve this dish in small bowls on jasmine or coconut rice.

PAD KRAPAO GAI

Working time approx. 20 minutes
cooking / baking time approx. 5 minutes
Total time approx. 25 minutes

ingredients
200 g chicken breast or other chicken meat
4 clove(s) of garlic
3 chili pepper(s) (Thai chili peppers)
1 tablespoon fish sauce
½ tablespoon soy sauce, light
1 tablespoon soy sauce, dark
½ tablespoon sugar or palm sugar
½ Handful of Thai Basil
1 egg
100 jasmine rice

Preparation
It is very important that all ingredients are prepared, as the actual cooking process is very fast. It is
advisable to prepare the rice before you start, as the
dish tastes best when fresh and warm.

Prepare the rice according to the instructions.

Cut the chicken into bite-sized pieces. Peel the garlic. Clean the chilies. Use a mortar to grind the garlic and the chillies until only small shreds are left. There should be no paste, just the garlic and chillies should be well chopped and mixed. Mix the sauces and the sugar in a small container.

Preheat a wok on the highest setting and heat about 3 tablespoons of oil. Beat the egg in and fry for about 30 seconds. While doing so, pour some of the hot oil over the egg again and again instead of turning the egg. The yolk should still be slightly liquid. Remove the egg from the wok and half of the remaining oil as well.

Now pour the garlic-chili mixture into the wok, stir briefly and add the chicken meat directly. Fry while stirring constantly until the meat is almost done. Stir the sauces again and add to the meat. Continue frying for about one minute. If the dish becomes very dry at this point, you can help it out with a sip of water.

Now remove the wok from the heat. Add Thai basil and stir in. The remaining heat is completely sufficient to heat the basil.

Place the rice on a plate, add the egg on top and the meat on the side.

SATÉ SKEWERS WITH CHICKEN

Working time approx. 30 minutes
Rest period approx. 2 hours
Total time approx. 2 hours 30 minutes

ingredients
500 g chicken breast fillet
1 tablespoon honey
60 ml sauce (Teriyaki sauce)
2 teaspoons oil (sesame oil)
1 teaspoon turmeric
1 teaspoon coriander, ground
½ teaspoon chili powder
1 small onion(s)
1 tablespoon of oil
150 g peanut butter, granular
2 tablespoons of sauce (Teriyaki sauce)
125 ml coconut cream
2 tablespoons chili sauce, sweet

Preparation
Halve the chicken breast fillets lengthwise and cut

into long thin strips. Put them on wooden sticks soaked in cold water (!) and stick them in an accordion shape.

Whip honey, teriyaki sauce, sesame oil, turmeric, coriander and chili powder into a marinade and marinate the skewers in it for at least 2 hours - but better overnight.

Sauté the onion in the oil until translucent, add the remaining ingredients and simmer at low heat to a creamy sauce.

Drain the skewers and either fry them in oil in a pan for about 5-7 minutes or grill them. Serve with the warm saté sauce.

Alternatively you can serve it as finger food on the cold buffet

SPICY BEEF SALAD

443 kcal
Working time approx. 40 minutes
Rest period approx. 2 hours
Total time approx. 2 hours 40 minutes

ingredients
550 g beef (beef rump)
3 tablespoons soy sauce
2 tablespoons fish sauce
2 tablespoons sugar, brown
3 clove/s of garlic, finely chopped
1 tablespoon ginger, fresh, finely chopped

For the sauce:
3 clove/s of garlic
6 chili pepper(s), e.g. jalapenos, with or without
seeds or less, depending on the spiciness
4 ½ tablespoon sugar, brown
3 tablespoons fish sauce
3 tablespoons lemon juice, freshly squeezed

For the salad:
1 head of lettuce, use the whole cleaned leaves
1 cucumber(s), peeled and thinly sliced

12 cherry tomato(s), halved, alternatively 3 bottle
tomatoes sliced
12 peppermint leaves, (as desired)
1 small onion(s), red, thinly sliced
4 g coriander green
40 g peanuts, roasted, roughly chopped

Preparation
Cut the meat in half, but do not cut it all the way
through, so that a thin, flat steak is formed. Cut the
meat crosswise on both sides with a sharp knife. The
cut should be about 5 mm deep. Place the meat in a
bowl or casserole dish.

For the marinade, mix soy sauce, fish sauce, sugar,
garlic and ginger in a small bowl. Pour the marinade
over the meat and leave to marinate covered in the
refrigerator for a minimum of 2 to maximum of 8
hours, turning the meat from time to time.

For the salad dressing, mix the garlic, chillies, sugar,
fish sauce and lemon juice in a mortar or blender to
form a paste.
Clean the lettuce and place the washed and well
drained leaves on a large plate or platter. Arrange
the cucumber slices on top of the lettuce as well as
the halved cherry tomatoes or bottle tomato slices.
Spread onions, plucked peppermint leaves and coriander green on top.

Heat up the grill for direct grilling. Remove meat
from marinade, dab dry. Brush and oil the grill rack,

place the steak on the hot grill rack and cook as desired (3-5 min. per side for a bloody to medium grilled steak). Put the steak on a plate to cool down (the meat should be served lukewarm). Then cut the steak into narrow strips diagonal to the grain.

Spread dressing over the salad and place the meat strips on top. Serve sprinkled with chopped peanuts.

MASSAMAN CURRY

Working time approx. 20 minutes
cooking / baking time approx. 20 minutes
Total time approx. 40 minutes

ingredients
500 g chicken breasts
1 bunch spring onion(s), approx. 3 - 4 pieces, depending on size
1 bag of curry paste (Massaman) is available in the asian store, 1 bag = approx. 3 tablespoons)
400 ml coconut milk
2 tablespoons peanut butter, creamy
1 tablespoon of sugar
1 tablespoon vinegar
4 tablespoons fish sauce
100 g peanuts, according to taste also less
4 medium-sized potato(es)
3 cm ginger, fresh
½ bunch coriander, fresh
1 stem lemongrass
Oil, for frying

Preparation

Cut the chicken breast into fine strips, cut the spring onions into rings, peel the potatoes and cut them into cubes of about 1 cm, peel the ginger and chop it very finely, cut the stem of lemon grass into three pieces.

Chop the coriander as well, while roughly separating the stems and possibly the roots (if they are not included in every bunch of coriander, they can be eaten without hesitation) from the leaves. This doesn't have to be absolutely exact, I just cook the stems and roots longer so that they become soft.

Heat the oil in a wok and fry the meat strips in it. Add the potato cubes and fry briefly. Deglaze with the coconut milk. Add curry paste, peanut butter, sugar, vinegar, fish sauce, peanuts, ginger, lemon grass, stalks and roots of coriander and cook for about 40 minutes stirring frequently. If too much liquid evaporates or the potatoes bind the curry too strongly, add some more water or broth if necessary.

At the end of the cooking time, fish out the lemongrass, add the spring onions, simmer for another 5 minutes, then add the coriander green and serve.

THAI GLASS NOODLE SALAD - YAM WOON SEN

348 kcal
Working time approx. 20 minutes
cooking / baking time approx. 10 minutes
Total time approx. 30 minutes

ingredients
1 tablespoon of oil
250 g minced meat, lean from pork, chicken or small, cooked peeled shrimps
3 tablespoons broth
6 tablespoons lime juice
4 tablespoons fish sauce
1 tablespoon chili paste, roasted (Nam Prik Paw)
1 cm ginger, finely chopped
3 clove/s of garlic, finely chopped
6 shallot(s), red Thai or small red onions
5 spring onion(s), Thai, alternatively 2-3 European
2 stalks of celery, Thai, alternatively 2 stalks of European

100 g glass noodles
2 tablespoons coriander green, roughly chopped, with stems
Lettuce
possibly peanuts
possibly chili pepper(s), chopped

Preparation
Scald the glass noodles with boiling water, leave to stand for 10 minutes, then drain well. Cut into 5 cm long pieces. Peel the onions and cut the celery and spring onions into thin slices.

Heat the oil, fry the garlic and ginger in it, do not brown. Then add the minced meat, fry briefly and deglaze with the broth. Cook for 2 - 3 minutes, crumble the minced meat roughly. Mix fish sauce, lime juice and chili paste, pour over the meat and continue cooking for a short time until the meat is cooked. There is no cooking time for cooked shrimp. Just mix them in and warm them up briefly.

When slightly cooled, mix into the noodles and vegetables. Fold in herbs and arrange on salad leaves. If desired, sprinkle with chopped chili and/or peanuts and garnish with some coriander.

FAST THAI CURRY WITH CHICKEN, PAPRIKA AND A FINE PEANUT NOTE

890 kcal
Working time approx. 30 minutes
cooking / baking time approx. 25 minutes
Total time approx. 55 minutes

ingredients
500 g chicken breast fillet, in fine strips
2 tablespoons vegetable oil
1 tablespoon soy sauce
1 ginger root, fresh, about the size of your thumb, peeled, finely chopped
1 tablespoon curry paste, red, or less
1 tablespoon peanut butter
400 ml coconut milk, unsweetened, creamy

2 bell bell pepper(s), red, in fine strips
3 spring onion(s), in fine strips
1 glass of bamboo shoot(s), in strips, well drained
10 corn calves, from glass, l.s. halved
1 tablespoon fish sauce
1 teaspoon palm sugar, alternatively brown sugar
1 teaspoon lemon grass paste or finely chopped lemon grass
1 tablespoon Thai basil, fresh
500 g jasmine rice or scented rice

Preparation

Mix the meat well with 1 tablespoon of oil, soy sauce and ginger and marinate for about 30 minutes. In the meantime, clean and cut the vegetables. Quickly fry the meat in a coated pan and then set aside.

Fry the curry paste in 1 tablespoon of oil in a wok or a large pan with a high rim. Stir in the peanut butter and let it melt. Deglaze with coconut milk, add the vegetables and let everything simmer for about 15 minutes.

In the meantime prepare the rice and let it steam.

Shortly before the end of the cooking time (the vegetables should still have bite) add the meat and heat it up again briefly. Season the curry to taste with palm sugar, fish sauce (if necessary take some salt) and lemongrass paste (should not cook). Sprinkle Thai basil on top and serve with the rice.

The composition of the vegetables can be varied/ added according to taste and availability, e.g. finely chopped water chestnuts for even more bite, a few small broccoli florets or some sugar snap peas (divided diagonally, blanched briefly or fried) as an additional splash of color. There should be a total of about 4-5 handfuls of vegetables (measured cleaned and cut).

Lemon grass paste is grated lemon grass soaked in a little vegetable oil. It is best to store the opened jar in the freezer.

THAI COCONUT SOUP WITH CHICKEN

Total time approx. 15 minutes

ingredients
½ Liters of coconut milk
½ Liters of chicken broth or vegetable broth, instant
4 Kaffir lime leaves
2 stems lemon grass
2 tablespoons curry paste, green
10 cm galangal or ginger
2 chili pepper(s) (Thaichili)
500 g chicken breasts
100 g mushrooms (shiitake) or mushrooms
2 tablespoons fish sauce
2 tablespoons cane sugar
4 spring onion(s)
1 handful of coriander
½ Lime(s), including the juice
possibly vegetables of your choice
possibly basil (Thai basil)

Preparation
Heat the broth together with the coconut milk and curry paste. Meanwhile peel and slice the galangal. Wash and halve lemon grass well, beat the thick ends with a meat tenderizer or a pan to bring out the aromas. Cut lime leaves into fine strips. Add everything to the coconut stock and simmer gently for about 10 minutes.

In the meantime, halve the chillies, remove seeds and cut into fine strips. Cut chicken, mushrooms and vegetables into bite-sized pieces. Fish lemongrass out of the soup and add the just cut ingredients. Simmer again for 10 - 15 minutes until everything is cooked.

Season with fish sauce, sugar and the juice of the lime. Arrange the soup and garnish generously with the plucked herbs.

THAI CURRY

679 kcal
Total time approx. 30 minutes

ingredients
500 g turkey breast fillet
1 bell bell pepper(s), red
1 onion(s)
1 garlic clove(s)
1 zucchini
1 large carrot(s)
200 g mangetout(s)
1 can of coconut milk
Curry paste, red
Sambal Oelek
Soy sauce
Basmati
Flour
Oil
Salt

Preparation
Cut the turkey meat into bite-sized pieces. Make a marinade from 3 tablespoons of oil, 2 teaspoons of red curry paste and 1 tablespoon of soy sauce. Marin-

ate the turkey meat for about 30 minutes (or longer), then dust some flour over the meat. In the meantime, chop all vegetables into small pieces.

Place the meat in a pan and fry until crisp, then remove.

Sauté the onion and the clove of garlic in the frying fat until translucent, then add the rest of the vegetables. Steam with lid for about 10 minutes, stirring occasionally. Now add a little water and add 2 tablespoons of the red curry paste and a good pinch of Sambal Oelek to the vegetables. Simmer for another 15 minutes, season with salt.

Then add the roasted turkey meat, stir in the coconut milk, bring to the boil again and remove the pan from the oven. If the sauce tastes too much like coconut milk, it can be diluted with broth or water.

Basmati rice goes well with this.

TOM KHA GAI - THE FAMOUS CHICKEN SOUP WITH COCONUT MILK AND GALANGAL

Working time approx. 30 minutes
cooking / baking time approx. 25 minutes
Total time approx. 55 minutes

ingredients
2 can/s of coconut milk à 400 ml
¼ Liters of chicken broth
5 stems lemon grass
7 cm Galangal, peeled, in slices
3 chili pepper(s), whole, red
3 tablespoons fish sauce
8 Kaffir lime leaves (Bai Magrood)

400 g chicken breasts, cut into small cubes or strips
150 g mushrooms, quartered (or fresh straw mushrooms)
2 lime(s), the juice
fish sauce, to taste
1 teaspoon palm sugar, possibly a little more (or refined sugar)

For the set:
Coriander green, abundant
5 spring onion(s) (Thai), in 2 cm long pieces
2 chili pepper(s), red, without seeds, cut into fine strips

Preparation
Cut the lemongrass into 4 cm pieces and tap them lightly with the back of a knife. Bring the broth and half of the coconut milk to a boil, add the lemon grass, galangal, Magrood leaves and chilies, season with the fish sauce and simmer for 10 minutes.

Add the mushrooms and cook for another 5 minutes, then add the chicken meat and cook for a few minutes on a low heat, it must remain tender. Add the remaining coconut milk and season with lime juice, sugar and fish sauce. Arrange in bowls and garnish with chili strips, spring onions and coriander.
The soup should taste freshly sour and slightly salty.

variants:
Replace chicken with 500 diced fish fillet, or 500g mushrooms.

Sea fish with firm meat or catfish and pike-perch are suitable as fish, if you prefer a more delicate fish taste.

STUFFED THAI OMELET

Working time approx. 20 minutes
cooking / baking time approx. 20 minutes
Total time approx. 40 minutes

ingredients
For the filling:
1 tablespoon of oil
150 g minced meat, lean, from pork
6 cherry tomato(s), quartered
1 onion(s), diced
5 small clove(s) of garlic, finely chopped
6 spring onion(s) (Thai spring onions), cut into rings, alternatively 3 normal spring onions
2 tablespoons coriander green, roughly chopped, with stems
125 g mung bean seedlings, coarsely chopped
1 chili pepper(s), red, seeded and finely chopped, more if desired
1 tablespoon fish sauce
1 tablespoon oyster sauce, possibly 2 tablespoons
1 teaspoon palm sugar, grated

Pepper, black
some lime juice
For the omelettes:
2 tablespoons of oil
4 eggs
2 teaspoons fish sauce

For the set:
2 tablespoons coriander green, plucked leaves
1 pepperoni, red (Thai pepperoni), seeded and cut into narrow strips

Preparation
Heat 1 tablespoon of oil in a wok, fry the garlic, onion and the chopped chilli pepper, add the minced meat, crumble it with a wooden spoon and fry it for about 5 minutes until it is lightly browned. Then season with fish sauce, oyster sauce, palm sugar, pepper and lime juice. Stir in the spring onions, tomatoes and sprouts and let it cook for another 1 - 2 minutes. Finally mix in the coriander. Set aside.

For the omelettes, whisk the eggs without too much foam and season with fish sauce.

Heat 1 tablespoon of oil in a large coated pan and pour in half of the egg mixture. Lower the temperature to a mild medium heat and let it slowly fade. When the omelette only shines on the surface, put half of the minced meat mass in the middle.
Then carefully fold the omelette over from all four sides to the middle to form a square. Turn over onto

a plate, from there slide onto a preheated plate and keep warm. Prepare the second omelette in the same way.

Add to the first one on the plate and garnish with coriander and chili strips.

Serve with fragrant rice.

THAI CURRY WITH CHICKEN, SNOW PEAS AND MANGO

Working time approx. 40 minutes
cooking / baking time approx. 25 minutes
Total time approx. 1 hour 5 minutes

ingredients
1 kg chicken breast
Milk
Cornstarch
1 mango
1 bunch spring onion(s)
400 g mangetout(s)
5 carrot(s)
1 garlic clove(s)
1 small onion(s)
some ginger root
Rapeseed oil

1 can/s of coconut milk
Curry paste, red or yellow
Curcuma
Cayenne pepper
salt and pepper
Sugar

Preparation
Cut the chicken breast into pieces and soak in a little milk with cornflour for about 3 hours.

Finely dice garlic and ginger. Cut snow peas, carrots, mango, spring onions and the onion into bite-sized pieces.

Brown the meat in a pot in some rape oil and then put it in the oven at approx. 160°C top/bottom heat, covered.

Fry the garlic, onions, ginger and spring onions in the wok with a little curry paste. Add the carrots and fry them a little more, then add the mangetout.
Add the meat from the oven to the vegetables, then also add the mango. Add the coconut milk, bring to the boil and season to taste.

Serve with rice.

THAI CURRY WITH PRAWNS AND SWEET POTATOES

Working time approx. 30 minutes
cooking / baking time approx. 15 minutes
Total time approx. 45 minutes

ingredients
2 medium sweet potato(es)
1 broccoli
350 g mushrooms or Asian mushrooms of your choice
200 g mangetout(s)
400 g shrimp tails
½ Bunch of Thai Basil
400 ml coconut milk from a can
200 g coconut cream
1 tablespoon curry paste, green
50 ml fish sauce, alternatively soy sauce possible
1 tablespoon of oil (peanut-)
Salt
Ginger powder

Coriander powder
Cumin

Preparation
Defrost frozen shrimp tails.
Peel, halve and slice the sweet potatoes. Wash the broccoli and cut into small florets. Clean and quarter the mushrooms. Wash and clean the mangetout and cut in half if desired. Wash the Thai basil and chop coarsely.

Heat the peanut oil in a large pan. Add the sweet potato pieces and steam for about 5 minutes, add a dash of coconut milk and the fish sauce. Stir in the curry paste. Add the broccoli florets and snow peas, steam briefly, add the rest of the coconut milk and the coconut cream. Now cook the prawns, mushrooms and Thai basil in the boiling sauce for about 5 minutes until the prawns and sweet potatoes are done.

Season to taste with salt, ginger powder, coriander and cumin.

GAI JANG - THAI GRILLED CHICKEN

Working time approx. 20 minutes
Rest period approx. 12 hours
cooking / baking time approx. 15 minutes
Total time approx. 12 hours 35 minutes

ingredients
1 kg chicken thigh, boneless

For the marinade:
4 tablespoons soy sauce
4 tablespoons fish sauce
4 tablespoons honey
2 tablespoons palm sugar or brown sugar
1 tablespoon coriander root(s), very finely chopped
1 tablespoon chili flakes
1 tablespoon turmeric (turmeric), ground

For the dip:
some tamarind paste, 2 tablespoons of water, should
be about as thick as tomato juice
2 tablespoons fish sauce
2 tablespoons lime juice

1 tablespoon chili flakes
½ tablespoon rice, light brown roasted and ground
1 clove/n garlic
1 tablespoon coriander green, chopped
1 tablespoon spring onion(s), chopped
1 teaspoon palm sugar or brown sugar

Preparation
Mix all ingredients for the marinade. Tap the chicken legs flat and put them in a freezer bag. Leave to marinate for a few hours or overnight.

Then fry over medium heat on a hot grill until the legs are done. Turn regularly.

In the meantime, mix the ingredients for the dip 'Nam Jim Gai Jang' and serve the chicken with it.

PEANUT SAUCE

590 kcal
Total time approx. 10 minutes

ingredients
400 ml coconut milk
1 tablespoon curry paste, red, heaped
125 g peanuts, unsalted, roasted
2 tablespoons palm sugar, grated
1 tablespoon fish sauce
2 tablespoons lime juice, or a little more preparation
Do not crush the peanuts too finely in the mortar,
there should still be pieces left.

Heat 3 tablespoons of the thick coconut cream, add
the curry paste and fry over medium heat for one
minute. Stir constantly with a whisk. When the
paste starts to smell, stir in the remaining coconut
milk, palm sugar, ground peanuts and fish sauce and
cook the sauce over a low heat for 10-15 minutes
until it thickens. Finally, season with lime juice and
possibly a little salt.

Serve lukewarm or cold.

PANÄNG MOO

Total time approx. 25 minutes

ingredients
2 tablespoons curry paste (Panäng Curry paste)
500 g pork or chicken (e.g. chicken breast, pork cutlet...), finely chopped
1 bag/s of coconut milk (approx. 200 ml)
3 tablespoons fish sauce
1 bunch basil (Thai basil)
4 Kaffir-lemon leaves
1 cup of water
2 carrot(s)
1 bell bell pepper(s)
1 teaspoon of sugar
1 tablespoon peanut butter or
Peanuts, powdered
possibly chili pepper(s)
possibly water

Preparation
Panäng Gai/Moo is an easy to cook, typical Thai recipe and contains fish sauce. Therefore no further salt is needed, because it is already very salty. But you should not be afraid of this ingredient, because

the dish will not taste like fish afterwards (at least it should).

In general, non-Thai people should be a bit more careful with the ingredients, because there are many (for the western palate) unusual tastes. Moreover, many of the ingredients in this recipe are already contained in some curry pastes.

It is therefore better to take a little less of the curry paste and fish sauce the first time than too much. If you notice afterwards that it was too little, you can add a little more just before the end (the ingredients dissolve wonderfully in the dish). If it is too much and the dish is too curry or salty, you can easily make up for it by adding a little more coconut milk and a small shot of water (for this purpose it is worth having a second pack of coconut milk in the house for emergencies).

And with the curry paste from Asian import stores you should always be careful: These usually already contain chili, which when cooked can produce a pungency that is unbearable for the western palate (and sometimes with a quantity of only 2 table-spoons!). I think it's better to take a curry paste without chili (German supermarkets sometimes have such a thing), because you can re-sharpen it with fresh Thai chilies at your own discretion. This also results in a more pleasant fruity pungency than the curry paste.

In general: Often try and season while cooking, then there is no bad surprise afterwards.

Fry the meat in a large pan until it is done. Then take the meat out of the pan and put it aside in a bowl (it will be used again later). Now pour the coconut milk into the large pan with the gravy (it is advisable not to pour all the coconut milk directly into the pan, but to keep a small part). Heat the coconut milk over medium heat until it simmers very slightly (do not boil!).

Now add 2 tablespoons of the curry paste to the coconut milk and stir until the paste has dissolved in the milk (do not leave any lumps, possibly reduce the heat). Keep stirring and add the 3 tablespoons of fish sauce to the curry coconut milk. Stir everything to a homogeneous mass and put the meat from the bowl back into the pan. Then heat it up a little bit (the meat should be warm).

Now cut the carrots into slices and the peppers into cubes. Pluck the leaves of the Thai basil and if necessary pluck them a little bit (do not chop them with a knife!) and put everything into the pan. If you like, you can now add 1 - 2 finely chopped chillies.

Either cut the lemon or kaffir leaves in half or wrap them in a roll (a prune) and cut them into very thin strips with a sharp knife. It depends on whether you like these lemon leaves so much that you want to eat them with you or whether you prefer to pick them out like bay leaves before eating and put them aside. Actually, the leaves only serve to give the food a fresh lemony scent, similar to putting bay leaves in a sauce or soup. However, I find them to be a very interesting flavor component, because they are - in contrast to laurel - not bitter! You can also put these leaves in the pan.

Now put a lid on the pan for 3 - 4 minutes until the vegetables have heated up a little. But it should still be crisp. Remove the lid, examine the whole thing and season to taste.

The dish is now almost ready, only the finishing touches are missing. For this you add a teaspoon of sugar. If the whole thing is very salty, you can also use a tablespoon of sugar. If it is too dry, add a little coconut milk and a shot of water. Now add the peanut butter or peanut powder and stir well once again. The dish should have only a fine peanut note, therefore only the small amount of 1 - 2 tablespoons.

Voilà ready is the Panäng. If pork is used, it is Panäng Moo, with chicken it is Panäng Gai. Basmati rice is the best side dish.

By the way, the vegetables are interchangeable. You could just as well add peas, mangetout, baby corn or something similar. Some people do it completely without vegetables, just with Thai basil. In my opinion, the only important thing is that you associate the vegetables with Asia (I wouldn't use vegetables like corn, tomatoes etc., that's more typical western style).

In Thailand it is not common to put salt and pepper on the table. One serves a small bowl in which 3 tablespoons of fish sauce, a good teaspoon of sugar and a thinly sliced Thaichili are mixed together. This salty-hot sauce is used to season the dish.

PINEAPPLE - SAUCE

Total time approx. 15 minutes

ingredients
2 chili pepper(s), red, seeded, chopped
1 bell pepper(s), yellow, cleaned, chopped
5 garlic clove(s), peeled, chopped
300 g pineapple, fresh, net, chopped
4 tablespoons vinegar, rice or coconut vinegar
½ teaspoon of salt, perhaps a little more
125 g sugar, possibly more

Preparation
Steam red chilies, peppers and garlic for 5 minutes or sauté on low heat in a pot while stirring, then mash in a mortar together with the pineapple or puree with a blender or wand until a paste is formed. Bring to the boil with 3-4 tablespoons of water, add the remaining ingredients and simmer until the mixture is syrupy. Then let it cool down.
The sauce should taste fruity-sweet-sour with a recognizable salt note. In no case like a dessert sauce.

It can be kept in the refrigerator for about 3 months.

Note:
If you like the sauce hotter, add the chilies with seeds to the sauce, or just a few seeds.

PAPRIKA - COCONUT - CURRY WITH TURKEY AND RICE

Total time approx. 25 minutes

ingredients
1 cup/s of rice (preferably sticky, but tastes good with everything)
3 cup/s of water
1 bunch spring onion(s)
1 bell pepper(s), red
½ Can of bean sprouts
5 garlic clove(s)
200 g turkey meat (fillet or similar)
some salt
Soy sauce
Curry paste, red
Ginger
Coriander

Basil, fresh
Chili
½ Can/s of coconut milk

Preparation
Depending on the working speed, you should also bring the water to the boil. As soon as it boils, reduce the flame, add rice and a teaspoon of salt, stir briefly and let it swell at very low heat without stirring further. After 10 - 15 minutes the rice is ready.

Strain the bean sprouts, wash and drain.

Wash the meat, dab dry and cut into bite-sized strips. Clean and wash the spring onions and cut them into approx. 1 cm wide pieces. Remove the seeds from the bell bell pepper and cut into small cubes, rhombs or strips. Finely chop the garlic, sprinkle salt over it and crush it a little with a spoon.

Now heat some oil in a hot wok and fry the meat. Add the garlic-salt mixture and a teaspoon of red curry paste shortly afterwards and let everything fry for a while. Now add paprika and spring onions to the wok and fry them as well. Do not forget the bean sprouts and add them to the wok. Meanwhile, the meat should be pushed to the edge.

Now deglaze with approx. 1 tablespoon of soy sauce and the coconut milk. As soon as the coconut milk is hot, you can start to season to taste.

For this I recommend some coriander, ginger and

chili (dry form) and if more pep is required, add more of the hot curry paste. Add more salt rather with soy sauce than with salt. If you have fresh basil, you should add the leaves after cooking. If you only have dry basil in stock, you can add it now.

Let it boil again briefly, arrange it and eat it.

THAI LYCHEE CURRY

Total time approx. 25 minutes

ingredients
400 g roast pork, thinly sliced or shredded
1 can of lychee / lychees, drained and halved, store juice
1 can of coconut milk
2 bell bell pepper(s)
1 teaspoon curry paste, red
Basil or Thai basil, some leaves thereof
1 onion(s)
some oil (sesame oil), or similar

Preparation
Chop the onion finely, sauté in hot oil, add the meat (important: on highest heat). Deglaze the whole thing with the juice of the lychees from the can, add the curry (dose according to the desired spiciness) and add the coconut milk in a few steps. Reduce the whole thing a little bit. Then add the peppers cut into small pieces (strips are ideal) and shortly after-

wards add the halved lychees. Boil them only briefly.

On the plate, add some (Thai) or normal basil to the garnish.

LIGHT CHICKEN CURRY WITH LEMONGRASS

Total time approx. 30 minutes

ingredients
500 g chicken breasts
1 mango, ripe (preferably flying mango)
1 can of coconut milk
100 g cashew nuts, (not salted)
1 lime(s)
4 small chili pepper(s), red
2 shallot(s)
2 clove(s) of garlic
1 piece ginger root, fresh
1 piece of galangal root or galangal powder
1 stick/s of lemongrass
1 bunch coriander, fresh
1 tablespoon of sugar
2 tablespoons chicken broth, instant
1 tablespoon fish sauce
2 tablespoons oil, (peanut oil)

Preparation

Cut chicken breast fillet into fine strips.
Roast cashew nuts in a pan while stirring constantly until golden brown (without oil), then put aside.

Peel ginger and galangal root and grate finely. Chop shallots and garlic very finely. Cut the chilies and lemon grass into small rings. Squeeze the lime.

Heat the oil in a wok. Sauté the shallots, garlic, chillies, ginger, galangal and lemongrass for approx. 1-2 min. while stirring constantly.

Add the meat, stir and fry briefly. Add the juice of the lime, sugar and fish sauce and stir. Pour in the coconut milk, add the chicken broth powder and simmer for about 15 - 20 minutes at low heat.

Shortly before the end of the cooking time, add the mango cut into cubes and the roasted nuts and let it simmer for another 5 minutes. Garnish with coriander after serving on the plate. If you do not like coriander, you can alternatively use basil, holy basil (Thai basil), or parsley, depending on your taste.

Goes well with this: Basmati or jasmine rice

THAI FISH FROM THE GRILL

Working time approx. 15 minutes
Rest period approx. 2 hours
cooking / baking time approx. 5 minutes
Total time approx. 2 hours 20 minutes

ingredients
1 kg fish fillet (e.g. redfish, hake, pangasius...)
1 tablespoon cumin
2 tablespoons oyster sauce
100 ml oil (e.g. sesame, sunflower or peanut oil)
1 teaspoon curry paste, green
½ Lemon(s), juice thereof
Salt
Sugar

Preparation
Salt the fillets and add a little sugar. Mix oil, oyster sauce, cumin, lemon juice and curry paste in a screw glass or shaker. The longer and more intensive you shake, the longer the marinade remains an emulsion.

Apply the marinade to the fish and leave the fish in

the fridge for at least 2 hours.

Then put it on the hot grill and grill it from each side for about 2 - 3 minutes.

Serve with rice or bread, white wine or beer.

SOUTH THAI CURRY WITH PRAWNS AND PINEAPPLE

1237 kcal
Working time approx. 20 minutes
cooking / baking time approx. 10 minutes
Total time approx. 30 minutes

ingredients
300 g shrimp(s), peeled, gutted, washed
2 tablespoons curry paste, red Thai, possibly less
60 ml fish sauce
500 ml coconut milk
200 g pineapple, fresh, pureed in a mixer
2 tablespoons palm sugar
60 ml lime juice, depending on the pineapple possibly less
1 handful of basil leaves (Bai Horapa), some of them as garnish

1 chili pepper(s), long, red, as garnish

Preparation

Take a large pot and boil up coconut milk, red curry paste, fish sauce and pineapple while stirring constantly. Add the prawns and lime juice and simmer for 3 - 5 minutes.

Add the basil leaves and the palm sugar (carefully, not the whole 2 tablespoons at first) and wait about 2 minutes until the flavours have combined. Season with fish sauce and, if necessary, more palm sugar.

Core the red long chili pepper and cut into very fine strips. Fill the curry into plates and garnish with chili strips and basil leaves, serve with rice.

THAI CHICKEN SWEET-SOUR

359 kcal
Working time approx. 15 minutes
cooking / baking time approx. 10 minutes
Total time approx. 25 minutes

ingredients
6 tablespoons of oil
500 g chicken breasts
2 tablespoons flour (alternatively corn flour)
1 onion(s)
1 bell bell pepper(s), green
6 tablespoons tomato ketchup
300 g pineapple pieces (small tin)
100 ml chicken broth
1 teaspoon soy sauce, sweet
1 teaspoon of sugar
1 dash of vinegar

Preparation
Cut chicken into small strips and turn in flour. Dice onion and paprika. Drain the pineapple.

Heat oil in wok or pan. Put the chicken in the wok and fry for about five minutes. Remove chicken from the wok with a ladle.

Add the onions and peppers to the wok and fry for two minutes. Add ketchup, pineapple, chicken stock, soy sauce, sugar and vinegar and stir-fry. Add the meat and cook for another two minutes.

PAD CHA WITH DIFFERENT SEAFOOD OR FISH

Total time approx. 20 minutes

ingredients
300 g shrimp(s), or fish or scallops or mixed seafood
1 tablespoon garlic
2 tablespoons shallot(s), Thai
5 chili pepper(s), red, finger length
5 spring onion(s), Thai
50 g ginger root (Krachai), fingerroot or Chinese. Ginger
30 g peppercorns, green, fresh, on the panicles
1 tablespoon fish sauce
1 tablespoon oyster sauce
1 tablespoon soy sauce, light
some sugar, to taste
80 ml broth, or water
1 handful Thai basil (Bai Gaprau)

Preparation

Fry prawns or other sea animals separately and keep warm.

Chop garlic, cut Thai shallots lengthwise into strips, chop chilies, chop spring onion, cut Krachai into thin rings or thin sticks, roughly divide green pepper (leave on panicles), pluck Bai Gaprau from stalks.

Heat oil in a pan or wok. Add onions and garlic and let it braise a bit, then add Krachai, chilies and green pepper and stir well. Deglaze with some stock, add fish, oyster and soy sauce, stir well. Season with sugar, add a little more fish sauce to taste.

Add shrimps or other seafood, spring onions and Bai Gaprau as well. Mix well and serve immediately over rice.

IMPRINT

Mindful Publishing

by
TTENTION Inc.

Wilmington - DE19806
Trolley Square 20c

Instagram: mindful_publishing
Contact: mindful.publishing@web.de

Printed in Great Britain
by Amazon

86060338R00068